Full of Feelings

Neha

Presentation by *BookLeaf Publishing*

Web: www.bookleafpub.com

E-mail: info@bookleafpub.com

ISBN: 9789395756280

First edition 2022

DEDICATION

I thank God almighty for his blessings, who created me and all of us.

This book is for my primary inspiration, my little daughter Myra and my husband Mahesh, my constant source of love, happiness and encouragement.

This book is for all members of Khairnar-Bhamre families, Grandparents, Narendra and Malti Bhamre (In-laws), Vijay and Anita Khairnar(Parents), and brother Kunal who support and motivate me in every aspect of my life.

This book is also for all relatives and friends who are there to help me whenever I need them.

Finally, this book is for all readers who will be part of my creative writing journey and I sincerely hope that readers will motivate me to write more of such creative work in the future.

ACKNOWLEDGEMENT

I would like to thank Bookleaf Publishing for their assistance and publishing this poetry book.

PREFACE

The poetry book 'Full of Feelings' is an outcome of a writing competition. This book was an attempt to write creative poems based on general ideas, imaginations, everyday stories, experiences and moments where everyone has experienced sometimes in their life.

The idea was very vague initially since the subject 'Feelings' itself is a limitless concept and there is tons of literature already there to read. I picked some specific feelings as a stepping stone for my poetry writing journey and explored the different styles, rhymes, schemes and kinds that help me to study poetic form and improve my writing. The poems included in this book are mostly free verse.

While making this book, the challenge was to find the sentiments in words which readers can feel from inside. It is a great adventure for any emerging writer like me to enhance the quality of content, specially this is about poems, where it has its own conventions and constraints over the language. While writing these poems, the intention was to cover the theme of both

negative and positive feelings within the
specification of competition.

During this journey, I was able to explore my
interests and engage in my hobby. Surely it was
exciting, trying to come up with a poem that
would please readers. For me in engineering
terms, poems were like software code of
emotions, where I needed to design, provide
input, write code, refactor if buggy and retest to
get an expected output, a great emotional poem
in the end.

Feelings

No one knows where feelings come from.
They might have forgotten by busy brains
Or hiding in the heart around deep dark walls.
Feelings seem realization of all senses
Which our brain handles smartly,
But could not understand, why the heart comes
Into the picture when it's about healing and
hearty.
Feelings are in desires, dreams, and epiphanies
Showing reflection of true self
They make us cry and laugh
admiring life In every moment
Feelings are about Humanness,
 the ability to feel and heal
Maybe we are so occupied running lifeless
wheel
Feelings are sadness, sorrow, and fears
Melting our hearts with love, affection, and tears
Maybe they make us weak, allowing sentiments
But there is happiness and joy to build our
strength
Our minds are powerhouses and thoughts
Are energies driven by those feelings `
Our life is all about hope, motivation, and
willing

We are In search of feelings approaching the
future
But unknown to what today is, hidden by nature
Feelings are the essence, the life of our soul
Without their presence, life is just a goal
Let's come back to life,
Understand its purpose and meaning
Because life is like a book,
 'Full of Feelings'!

Happiness

Happiness is there every day.
There at the window, the day is full of life,
waiting for you to fulfill your dreams and enjoy-
bright summers or lovely rainy days.
There in the kitchen, the empty cups are waiting
for you,
to pour some coffee into them and They can
fulfill -
purpose of being there for you
There will be the roads waiting for you,
to walk over them and lead your life in your own
way
There will be new adventures waiting for you
to feel yourself, Learn to cry and laugh -
no matter what yesterday was.
There will be lunch and dinner to enjoy
full of tasty food and flavors with people around
-
Maybe someone has made them think about you
or
Maybe a complete stranger with magic hands.
There will be some interesting moments at the
bus stop
and to meet strangers or leave the ones you
know

When you reach the gate of the office, no one
will be there -
to grit you but still be very happy to see you
from
the corner of the cubicle Or maybe someone will
not be pleased with all
but still will grit you "a very nice day"!
Somebody might say "Good job"," All the best",
"Nice to meet you" or even say "bugger off"!
There will be your family, friends, and children
waiting for you
to come home in the evening and hugged you
tightly
Like you never met each other
There will be some moments when you will get
angry
And depressed with tiring thoughts and a rolling
mind
But you still will smile and laugh at hearing
jokes
And watching funny TV series, enjoying the rest
of the evening
There will be 'Hi's and 'Byes' messages,
'good night' kisses and hugs from loved ones
that will make your day count.
The night will be waiting for you to sleep
so you can dream about the next day of your life,
Just like every day!

Blessed

She was so tiny,
Also full of hair,
Her skin was light,
Greasy and Fair..

Her heart was racing,
Also full of Fear,
Her eyes were closed,
Also full of Tears..

Her hands were shaking,
Her legs were stretching,
She was finally coming into our world,
With joy and blessings..

Her loud cry slows down a little,
When he holds her in his arms,
She was meeting her father,
And might felt his charms

She was still crying,
Looking for someone
with her closed eyes…
She was full of life,
And ready to live and rise..

I realized she was an Angel,
Searching for Heaven..
She was looking for Me..
because God blesses me
as a MOTHER!

Love

Love is in those tears, expressions of proud
    Carrying heart inside in unspoken words
Making sure you are safe in a crowd
    Grabbing your hand but free like birds

Love is in patience, understanding, and
motivation
    Forgiving mistakes without their consent
Realizing there is nothing based on any fact or
condition
    Taking care of each other is lifelong
presents

Love is in enchantment, excitement, and
melancholia
    The feeling of true companions, meeting
the soulmate
Trying hard to embrace, moving on with love
phobia
    Enjoying memories, let others throw on
the fate

Love is in the purpose of fulfillment, joy, and
happiness
    It is in commitments, friendship, and
never-ending kindness

Safe

The world out there,
Is Brutal..
But I know I am safe,
Because I am hiding in the world's safest place,
It's in your Arms..!

The world out there,
Is taking my test at every step..
But I know, I will not Fail,
Because I have won the race already
By knowing, you will be there, even if I fail..!

The world out there,
Is cursed..
But I know, I will not be affected,
Because I am living in the world's sacred place,
It's In your Heart..!

The world out there,
looking for my weaknesses..
But I know, I can fight against it,
Because I have world's biggest strength,
It's in your Love..!

The world out there
Is full of loneliness..
But I know, I will never be abandoned,
Because you will be there with me,
Now and Forever..!

Intimacy

It's a true blessing of God
Mating of two Souls,
Leading into another Life !
It's the Closeness at the Edge of the horizon,
Where Soil meets the Sky,
Even if they are at the farthest distance from
each other!
It's the Miraculous development of Affection,
between two unknowns,
Beginning to feel towards each other !
It's the Charming Fire,
Burning differences between two loved ones,
And making a New One!
It's in Mesmerizing Evening,
When Sun meets the Night,
To share the last day of Light !
It's in Magical Touches
Enchantment of two Hearts
To experience the feeling of Love !
It's in the Glorious Night
Embracing each other
To live one dream, Together !
It's the sensational Desire,
Need of an Attachment,
To fill each other's, Emptiness !

It's the Belongingness
Where nothing is about mine,
It's only about the 'US' !
It's all about Love,
It's all about Trust,
It's about commitments,
To stay together for Eternity!....

Joy

Child: "Mom, I want to find Joy !"
Mom: "Oh, who is he?"
Child: "My teachers said 'you have to find Joy
to be happy'
Mom: "Oh ok, can you find him behind the
door?"
Child: "no, nothing is there!"
Mom: "Hmm ok, search everywhere in the
house then, he surely will be somewhere"
The poor child searched every corner
of the house and found nothing.
She come with teary eyes and said,
"Mom, I think he left, I lost him."
Then her mother took her in her arms and started
tickling
The little child started laughing.
Soon forgot to cry and started singing
with her funny, loud voices and blabbering
words,
The whole house was noisy,
 Echoing with their funny giggles and laughs
"Now here it is, you got it, you have found the
JOY.
Joy is inside you, inside me, and how happy we
are!",

Her mother made her realize what JOY is all
about.
Joy is everywhere, you just need to find it. In
those
sweet little simple things, you can never
imagine.

Hope

I will be there with you,
Always ..
No matter how much darkness in there -
inside you or outside world
I will always enlighten you with my presence.
No matter how hard your life is -
Struggle for existence or maintaining the heights
I will always come around full of possibilities.
No matter how alone you think you are
Finding yourself in the crowds or exploring
loneliness -
I will always find you like a true companion.
No matter if whole world is against you
Friends, enemies or its you against you
I will always be by your side sharing your
ground.
No matter how good and best you are,
A rookie or skilled facing the difficulties in life
I will never let you down even at your worst.
No matter how depressed and purposeless you
think you are,
Oversleeping, sleepless or going through never
ending nightmares
I will never let yourself go and stop dreaming

No matter how much pain you are suffering
from an old scars or fresh wounds
I will become medicine even if it is incurable
No matter how big and uncountable mistakes
you have made,
May seemed unfair and unforgettable
But I will always be there to forgive and
motivate
You may feel the end of road when you took
wrong turn,
Destiny may be vanished or seemed unreachable
I will always be there to lead you to new turn
Your life may be counting the days for your last
moments
There may be sadness, grief and hurtful events
I will always cherish you with pleasing
memories
When you will be taking your last breath,
It may be the death of your life and end of your
soul
I will be there praying, hopeful for another life!

- I am Hope

Anxiety

"Will she be fine?"..
He was thinking about her while waiting in line..
"What if she needs anything?",
He looked around and started distracting himself towards other things..
"Her eyes were full of tears, I shouldn't have let her go..",
The bad thoughts were rolling in his mind and He started feeling low..
"What if she get lost and I will not able to bring her back",
He might have felt some Insecurities,Agitation, Sorrow and Lack..
"Each seconds seems like an year",
His heart was pounding with Worry and Fear..
"Hope.. she is alright!",
He was waiting at the gate like a soldier, Ready to Fight..
He passed his hours, Thinking about her
Looking at the doors with excitement and eager
The moment came.they opened the gates,
She ran towards him with arms open and full of grace
He lift her in his arm, Took a deep breath,

He close his eyes, Feel her happiness
She said, "Papa, I missed you",
He could not speak a word for seconds
Then said, "I miss you too, my dear!"
Today he realized
What it's like, feeling Anxiety,
It was her day at school
but his adventure is worrying..!
No one can imagine the Feelings of motherhood,
But today he was experiencing feelings of
Fatherhood!

Satisfaction

I am very soft and gentle,
Just like the cozy pillow in winter
Where everyone can lie their head and
sleep calmly without any fear of getting lost
I am harmonious like a cold breeze
With the mild scent of a flower where senses
will feel the aroma
and memorize those moments with special ones
And experience the love is in the air
I am so complete and mindful where
Anyone can feel the completeness and the
winner
of life leaving all enemies and odds behind
I am pure and graceful just like the clean water
of the river where anyone can fulfill their thirst
and experience the feeling of gratification
I am full of life and happiness,
Just like the feelings in baby cuddles
Where you never want to let go of those baby
arms
and tiny life in those hands
I am always there with hope and positivity
and no one can ever be alone.
I am always fulfilled with life,
making sure everyone's life is Fulfilled,

before closing their eyes.
I am 'Satisfaction',
the feeling of fulfillment.

Proud

It was a bright sunny day
He was walking with his mother,
Jumping on sidewalk
Looking around everywhere
Suddenly he saw,
A family of four,
Staying in a tent,
At the corner of the edge
He asked, "Mom, who are they"?
She replied," They are like us, but they don't
have a home"
He was looking at those children
Until His mom turned him to the garden
A lot of thoughts were running through his mind
Until the late evening,
The rain started with the storm warning
He ran to mom and asked,
"Mom look, there will be a storm
What will those homeless do?
Should I ask them to come to our home?
Just for today, Please?"
She smiled and replied,
"Yes, You can", and he ran outside.
She was looking at him proudly,
Wondering if she made a "Human"
with Humanity!

Silence

There are some voices you can hear around and
Let yourself understood by their presence
Words are not always meaningful and destined
to be
a true explanation of your feelings

Sometimes you have to let yourself drown in
chaos to
Feel the peace lies within yourself
Noises are not always loud and blasting,
they can be satisfactory too

Sometimes you just have to see around and let
yourself
pleased to see how things are different but
beautiful as well
Expressions are not always enough and adequate
to express the idea of speechlessness

Sometimes you just have to stay still and let
yourself
Free along with the flow
Responses are not always appropriate and
relevant
To provide significance of yourself

Sometimes you just have to stop and take a long
breath
Punctuations are not always there to stop you
and
To prepare you for your next sentences

Sometimes you just have to be silent to
understand
the language behind the words
And to recognize the strength in you to
lead your life with patience and peace!

Sadness

Sadness is in those overwhelming tears where
They come out because of strength of your
emotions
They hit the edge of your eyes so hard that there
will be
flood in your heart and your eyes speak more
than your words.
It's the pain you are going through is not because
of wounds with
the blood but because of unexpected invisible
cuts in your heart which
Will keep on bleeding unless you overcome it
with self-healing.
It's the pounding heart and shaking body when it
breaks
the silence of thoughts and brings the chaos with
lonely darkness of night
just like the highest tide of sea destroying the
life of the shore
It's in the scary unknown faces of knowns that
come out in
In the middle of the night and take your true self
unless you
Try hard and wake yourself by the conscious
mind

It's in the unaccepted failure of gains, trust, and
hard work
putting everything You have, awaiting for your
destiny to turn around
unless you make expectations to be unexpected.
It's in those self-pity habits satisfying the ego
and blame on
Situations and every aspect of failure just for
satisfying self-worthy
And defenses for every failure
It's the journey on silent roads with lots of
accidents,
Realizing and revealing unknown turns, edgy
hills and visionless
Fog unless you walk it over with a clear mind
Sadness is in everyday cribbing, losing every
other moment
And searching for moles in happy faces,
unaware about
Emotions are in the moment.
What comes out with sadness though?
Sadness teaches the strength to fight against it,
Patience with hope and realization of
What it's like to be Happy!

Jealousy

Jealousy is a Sprout,
Growing seeds of Toxicity,
It's bitterness Emotions,
Full of Negativity

Jealousy is a Reason,
For Hatred and Enmities,
It's a Burning Sensation,
With lots of Insecurities

Jealousy is a Mold,
Creating adverse Emotions,
Feelings of Mistrust,
Doubts and Suspicion

Don't look at the things
you don't own,
It will always feel less
Sad and Unknown

Jealousy can always lead
Hate and Distance
Loss of Companionship,
Dislikes and Resistance

"How can He be with,
Full of success and happiness?"
"How can she be with,
Full of beauty and grace?"

"How can she bless,
With love and satisfaction?"
How can he bless,
With romance and affection ?

"How can she gets easily
Whatever she desires?"
"How can he be so passionate
And ready to inspire?"

Everyone has their own Life,
Living on their own Ways
Everyone has their own Choices,
Leading Dark or Bright days

Confront your emotions
Cope with your fear,
Aware of your mind,
Let it clean and clear

Stop thinking about others,
Comparing your neighbors
You are the owner of your life
Be a Real Creator !!!

Dependency

Dependency is Fear,
Fear of Rejection,
Can I stand outside without anyone's
Assistance?
Dependency is Habit,
Habit of Reliance
Either for Emotional support Or Social
Compliance
Dependency is an Excuse,
Excuse, running from Hard work,
Because you need to work on Your Negatives
and Quirks
Dependency is a Weakness,
Weakness of can't be lonely,
It's a feeling of possessiveness and searching for
reasons for jealousy
Dependency is Belief,
The belief in emptiness without others,
It's an Unwilling Satisfaction, Even if it bothers
Dependency is a Dream,
Viewing from someone else's eyes
It's a persistent feeling of absence, Ignoring
truths behind lies
Dependency should be a Choice
Not a Requirement or a Necessity,

You should be able to lead your life
Not one's Responsibility or a Liability
Dependency is Not an Enemy,
Not even a Motivation to stay Alone
Because everyone needs hands,
To behold and To be owned
Dependencies comes along
with Love and Affection,
It should lead happiness
Not a Tension and Rejection
Encourage your Confidence
Build your Self Esteem
Open your eyes
And Live your own dreams
Drive your thoughts
Away from Insecurities,
Follow your passion
And fight your Anxiety
Be Independent
Build Self Worth,
Lead your Own Life
because You are Special from Birth!

'Demons' and 'Daemons'

The book of feelings was characterizing
different acumens
It made me curious about,
'Demons' and 'Daemons'.

The addition of a single syllable can make a
difference
Is this about their beliefs Or Just norms of
characters?
Are these truths residing in Mythological
creations?
Or are these cultural facts based on imagination?

'Daemons' are depicted as Blessed spirits,
Creating forms of Goodness
'Demons' are depicted as Evil spirits,
Driving force of Badness

'Daemons' seems an entity between gods and
humans,
It's a ghostly presence Between mortals and
immortals
'Demon' seems a force with power and
Intensity,

Its darkness in angels with supernatural
Malignancy

'Daemons' can be in sympathy, In affection, and
empathy,
It is silently there, securing our Humanity
'Demon' can be an Anger, we carry Inside,
It kills the heart and diminishes our soft side

'Daemons' begins with concerns, and ends with
kindness,
It passively argues, with the emotions of
stiffness
'Demons' begins with toxicity, securing grudges
inside,
It hinders in Lies so it can never be seen outside

'Daemons' can have powers in making
companions and friends,
Soften an enemy by the following selflessness
'Demons' carries weapons of Insults and
humiliation,
It rides abusive words as a defensive mechanism

'Daemons' might there to make a Love and
Peace,
Assisting families and orphans with loneliness
feelings

'Demons' come with children of Hate and
Aggression,
It comes with thoughts of Hostility and Intrusion

'Daemons' may be in willpower and our Inner
courage
Serving as a guardian angel against thoughts of
Rages
'Demons' comes out timely with Rage and
Temper,
It Rises with Provocation, Annoyance, and
Agitation

'Daemons' may be a trait of watching others at
difficult times,
It's the best version of humans with sense and
wise
'Demons' are skillful, turning Anger into
Violence,
It can turn a human Into a ruthless savage in
seconds

'Daemon' is protecting us at the gate of outburst,
Where thoughts drive us to avoid making it
worse
The world is under attack By the 'Demons'
inside us,
We need to fight them with inner strength and
self-trust!

'Demons' can't be destroyed,
'Demons' can't be vanished,
It can just be controlled by the 'Daemons',
fighting from our positive side!

Whatever they are,
Good or Bad,
They are in us,
May be created by god..!

Recognize them,
Drive them with your Courage
Understand their Presence
And
Live life with happiness and the sage ..!

Abandoned

I am waiting for someone,
from years and ages,
They abandoned me when some humans came in
rages

We were so happy,
enjoying full of life,
He was living inside me, with his kids and wife

They put soul in me,
made up of their love and heart,
We were meant to stay together and never be
apart

There used to be noises,
cries and healthy fights
Still, It was the joy and peaceful nights

They were making sure I was clean and
beautiful every day,
They were always caring and never left me away

One day night,
some humans came,
They warned his family with guns and blades

He took his family and
 put on some courage,
They wrapped their stuff overnight and filled
their carriage

I remembered the last night,
the moments and sorrow,
He looked at me and said, "he will be back
tomorrow"!

Just like the birds,
they can abandon the nest,
He left me like an orphan with sadness in his
chest

It's been years,
since they have disappeared,
No one comes to this side because its
abandoned, full of fear

Leftovers things are now my new friends,
With whom I spend my weeks and weekends

Loneliness is my mate never leave me alone
Felt useless,
helpless and thrown

I am just an "Abandoned House"

but I still can feel their presence,
They will come,
looking for me and I will have a family once
again !!!

Depression

Feelings were like ;
Falling into a deep dark Valley,
It was a never-ending path of Sadness Alley!
It was Fading and Dying every day,
But Death kept saying, it's on another day!

An interesting life turned into the Darkness,
No signs of lights and deep dark Sadness
Everything was gloomy and nothing felt
Around,
still was falling in the air and awaiting Ground

Finally reached somewhere the place never seen
Before,
Heard like water running, seems like a Shore
Feelings were Creepy with Anonymous's
Presence,
Everything around was Empty and asking for
Essence

Suddenly things around turned into fresh
Flowers,
It was a calm moonlight with slight rain and
Showers

Walked around everywhere and tried to find
Someone,
Someone should be there, an Enemy, Friend, or
Love one!

Things started moving again
Did not understand where and when?
Mind was playing a lot of Games
Was it an Illusion, Sadness, Grief, or blame?

This time there was no water, doom dry myriads,
Smelled like smokes, burns, and flashy bodies
Everything was burned like cities made up of
ashes,
My eyes cried like a flood and painful
whiplashes

Scared to death and ran like never run,
Reached at the tip of the cliff with thoughts,
"What have I done"?!
Then waited so long for a Sun to rise,
Waited for someone who will help and Wise

Suddenly things started moving Again,
Going through the similar wheel of Pain
 Saw past scary shadows coming like a Stormy,
Were they shadows or blackness buried in me?

This time I decided, I will not run with Sorrow
and Fear,
I will stand firm and face it, with little Hope, and
Revere
These bodies, these shadows are nothing but a
spiral of thoughts,
I will fight and control them even if they are
countless and in lots!

I waited till shadows covered me in their Black
Arms,
Then I fought like a warrior with Sparks and
Charms
It took a lot of strength to fight against own
Fear,
It needs a weapon of courage to drive Hope
Spear

Shadows were very stubborn and kept on
coming
I was also persistent, kept on fighting

Suddenly those shadows vanished,
and they pushed me from the cliff
It was not Falling,
but the Rising with Own Belief!

When senses come into life and

It opens up my real eyes
Then I realized I came out of Depression,
Leading A New Life !!!

Anhedonia

It's an interesting state of mind
where nothing seems interesting..
Its Detachment from life,
Without even realizing
Your Brain might ask you,
For an Agreement of Closure
To avoid Joyful Moments and Loss of Pleasure
It's like a Dead tree
Who does not have any Desire,
To create sweet Fruits or Flourish with Flowers
It is an act of staying Aloof and becoming
Careless
Not any feelings of Relief or
Not even any Stress
It's a Journey with no destination,
Going on an endless Track
It's an Emptiness and Ignorance,
Even if one Lost or Wrack
It's the Silent Ride,
With a mood of Highs and Lows
It's all passive thoughts,
Wherever Wind Flows
Don't need Friends,
Don't need Loved ones
Not even thoughts of enemies,

Wandering with Dead ones
It is basically a Trauma Or sort of Illness
It can be cured, With your power of Willingness!
Break the frozen Thoughts,
Unmute your Mind
Reclaim your Joy
By leaving Darkness Behind!

Grief

He might have woke up today
Without any Pain and Suffering,
He might have felt it
more than Unusual and Surprising!

He might have Experience
Intense Peace and Calmness,
Then he might have confused it
With Medicinal Dizziness!

He might feel very happy
to see all those faces around,
It must be Atypical and
Emotional Profound!

He might want to Express
 his Happiness and Feelings,
But seems everyone was busy
In one's Memorizing and Mourning

He might have looked back
Watched his dead body lying in a bed.
Then he might have realized,
He had no time
It was his 'Death'!

Deja Vu

Deja Vu..
A Strange feeling..
When you are living in moments,
But it feels like they have already 'Passed' !
A Flashback of Memories..
Randomly appearing in your Present,
Saying, "this is nothing but your 'Past'" !
French origin explained it,
As 'Already Seen'
It is a confrontation that once was a dream!
How one can possibly feel,
Such an extraordinary event?
Just like a time repeated wheel,
In seconds and segments..
It might be a God,
Resetting clocks inside our brain
I had been through this incident,
But somehow forget exactly when?
The one reading this poem
Might have already read,
Just like the cover of a book,
Opening from the end!
The one living this life
Might have already dead,
This is just an Illusion of the new Life ahead!

As per scientific explanation,
'The Parallel Universe' do exist out there,
Will, there be another you,
leading your life somewhere?
This also can be possible,
The brain is going through some setbacks
It experiencing emotional stresses,
Just like some system hacks
Maybe this brainy glitch
Is nothing but the chance,
A warning sign or indication,
To take a future glance
Whatever this is,
Seems really amazing,
This opens up some hope
To travel past life
I wish one day,
We will reveal this mystery,
So we can do better,
For the next life and history!
For now,
As a reader of this poem,
Think about,
What you want to do 'better' in life,
if you would have solved this mystery?
Today, You can't change the past,
But you still can make History!
The future is still in your Hands

Based on your Dedication, Motivation, and
View,
Because life is not all about,
just another DEJA Vu !